CONSTITUTION

OF THE

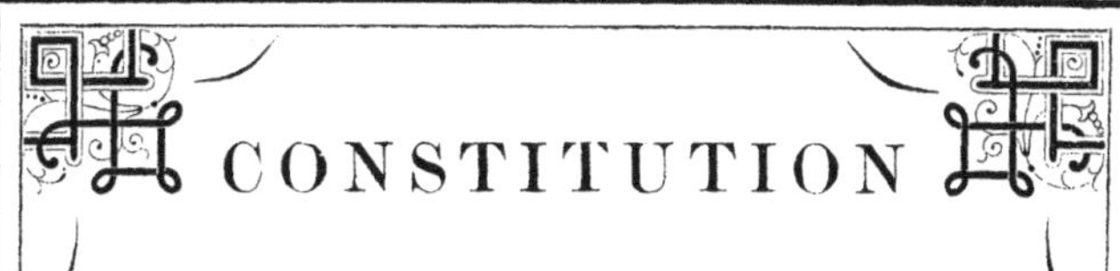

OF IOWA,

Adopted at Iowa City, February 7, 1857.

BY-LAWS

ADOPTED APRIL 7, 1869.

ARTICLES OF INCORPORATION

AND

LAWS OF THE STATE RELATING TO THE SOCIETY.

PRINTED AT THE IOWA TRIBUNE OFFICE,
IOWA CITY.

1869.

CONSTITUTION

OF THE

State Historical Society

OF IOWA,

Adopted at Iowa City, February 7, 1857.

BY-LAWS

ADOPTED APRIL 7, 1869.

ARTICLES OF INCORPORATION

AND

LAWS OF THE STATE RELATING TO THE SOCIETY.

PRINTED AT THE IOWA TRIBUNE OFFICE,
IOWA CITY.
1869.

CONSTITUTION

OF THE

State Historical Society of Iowa.

CHAPTER I.

NAME.

ARTICLE 1. This Organization shall be called the "State Historical Society of Iowa."

CHAPTER II.

MEMBERSHIP.

ART. 1. The members of this Society shall consist of those persons who are elected at any meeting of the Society, or by those officers authorized by this Constitution, and who have paid into its treasury the sum of three dollars admittance fee, and one dollar annually thereafter.

ART. 2. Individuals may be elected honorary members of this Association, who shall be entitled to all the privileges of regular members, except the right to vote and hold office, and shall be exempt from paying the annual fee of membership.

ART. 3. The members of this Society shall have free admission to its rooms and lectures, and the privilege of consulting its books, maps, charts, and papers.

CHAPTER III.

OBJECT.

ART. 1. The object of this Society shall be to collect, embody, arrange and preserve in authentic form, a library of books, pamphlets, maps, charts, manuscripts, papers, paintings, statuary and other materials illustrative of the history of Iowa; to rescue from oblivion the memory of its early pioneers; to obtain and preserve narratives of their exploits, perils and hardy adventures; to secure facts and statements relative to the history, genius, progress or decay of our Indian tribes, to exhibit faithfully the antiquities, and the past and present resources of the State; and to promote the study of history by lectures, and diffuse and publish information relating to the description and history of Iowa.

CHAPTER IV.

OFFICERS.

ART. 1. The officers of this Society shall be a President, six Vice Presidents, a Corresponding Secretary, a Recording Secretary, a Treasurer, Librarian, and eighteen Curators, who shall be chosen annually.

ART. 2. The President shall preside at the meetings of the Association, preserve order therein, and in case of an equal division of the members, give the casting vote.

Art. 3. Either of the Vice Presidents, in the absence of the President, may perform the duties of that office.

Art. 4. The Recording Secretary shall keep a record of each meeting of the Society, and submit the same for approval.

Art. 5. The Corresponding Secretary shall have charge of the correspondence of the Society, be a member of the Board of Curators, have a general oversight of all its affairs, subject to the direction of the Executive Officers, to whom he shall make a monthly report of all his doings; write the annual report, and be known as the official organ.

Art. 6. The Treasurer shall receive all dues and donations of money, pay all drafts drawn on him when signed by the President and Secretary of the Board of Curators, and keep a regular account of the financial concerns of the Society, and make a full and accurate report of the same, accompanied by satisfactory vouchers, to the Curators at their last regular meeting previous to the annual meeting of the Association.

Art. 7. The Curators, a majority of whom shall reside in the vicinity of the State University, and five of whom shall constitute a quorum, shall be the Executive Department of this Association, having full power to manage its affairs in harmony with this Constitution. They shall keep a full and correct account of all their doings, and make a report of the same, together with that of the Treasurer and Librarian of this Society, through the Corresponding Secretary, at each annual meeting, to be transmitted to the Governor, and be by him laid before the General Assembly, as required by the act making an annual appropriation to this Society. They shall also have the power, in the name of the State Historical Society of Iowa, for themselves and their successors in office, to sue and be sued, implead and be impleaded, defend and be defended in all courts and places, and for the purposes of this Association may do all such acts as are performed by natural persons.

ART. 8. In case any vacancies occur in the officers of this Society, the Board of Curators shall have power to fill such vacancies, and also to elect such members of the Society as they may deem best, and appoint a corresponding member in each county.

ART. 9. The annual meeting of this Society shall be held on the first Tuesday of December, at which time the officers for the succeeding year shall be chosen, and no member shall be eligible to an office, or be entitled to vote, who has not paid the annual fee of membership.

ART. 10. The Librarian shall have charge of the books, papers, maps, charts, and all other similar valuables of the Society, under the direction of the Board of Curators, to whom he shall make report as they may require, to be by them incorporated in the annual report to the Society.

CHAPTER V.

AMENDMENTS.

ART. 1. This Constitution may be amended at any meeting of the Society, when requested by the Board of Curators.

BY-LAWS

MEETINGS.

SECTION I. The regular meetings of the Board of Curators shall be on the first Wednesday in each month. The President of the Board shall order special meetings whenever he may deem it necessary, OR AT THE REQUEST OF THREE MEMBERS. The hour of such meetings shall be fixed by the Board from time to time.

SEC. II. In the absence of the President from any meeting, the Secretary OR ANY MEMBER MAY call the Board to order, and upon motion any member thereof may be chosen President pro tem.

SEC. III. Five members of the Board shall constitute a quorum for the transaction of business; but any less number may adjourn from time to time.

ORDER OF BUSINESS.

SEC. IV. The order of business of this Board shall be as follows:

1. The call of the roll of the Board.
2. The reading and approval of the proceedings of the previous meeting.
3. Communications.
4. Reports of Officers.
5. Reports of Standing Committees.
6. Reports of Special Committees.

7. Proposals for Membership.
8. Voting for Members.
9. Unfinished Business.
10. New Business.

STANDING COMMITTEES.

SEC. V. There shall be six "Standing Committees" of the Board, consisting of three members each, to be appointed by the President thereof, previous to the second meeting after his annual election, and designated as follows:

1. On Publication.
2. On Library Rooms.
3. On Finance.
4. On Natural History.
5. On Picture Gallery.
6. On Obituaries.

THEIR DUTIES.

SEC. VI. The Committee on Publication shall provide for the Publications of the Society from year to year; also, to procure the binding of all unbound books, pamphlets, magazines, newspapers, &c., from time to time, as the Board may direct.

SEC. VII. It shall be the duty of the Committee on Library Books to investigate from time to time the condition of the books, pamphlets, papers, maps, charts, pictures, cabinets and other articles in the Library Rooms of the Society; provide for their arrangement and preservation; also, to provide suitable rooms, with all necessary arrangements for the use of the Society, under the direction of the Board.

SEC. VIII. It shall be the duty of the Committee on Finance to examine all bills and claims against the Society; to investigate the affairs and accounts of the Secretary and Treasurer, whenever the Board may direct; also, to examine his annual report and accompanying vouchers, and if found correct, to endorse upon it their certificate of approval.

SEC. IX. It shall be the duty of the Committee on Natural History, to procure articles or specimens of any character, which will in their judgment, serve to illustrate "Natural History," and especially that of Iowa, and cause the same to be properly classified and arranged in its appropriate cabinets.

SEC. X. It shall be the duty of the Committee on Picture Gallery to procure and arrange, so far as possible, the portraits, or other class of pictures of such citizens of Iowa from its early settlement forward; and such other pictures and sketches of objects and scenes within this State, or elsewhere, as in their judgment may be suitable and worthy of such keeping and preservation.

SEC. XI. It shall be the duty of the Committee on Obituaries to prepare, or cause to be prepared, a proper and suitable obituary of each member of this Society, who may decease, for preservation and publication.

OFFICERS.

SEC. XII. At the first meeting of the Board, after the annual election of the Society, there shall be chosen from the members by ballot a "President of the Board of Curators," who shall hold his office for one year, and until his successor shall be duly elected. He shall preside at the Meetings of the Board, and preserve order therein.

SEC. XIII. The Corresponding Secretary of the Society shall be EX-OFFICIO Secretary of the Board of Curators. He shall keep the roll of membership of the Society, report all delinquents for dues of membership, and Annals' subscription, quarterly to the Treasurer, and report all moneys received by him to the Board monthly, and pay the same to the Treasurer.

Sec. xiv. The Treasurer of the Society shall give bonds in the sum of $3,000, to be approved by the Board, for the faithful performance of his duties, and shall collect all membership dues and subscriptions to the Annals, and report quarterly to the Board.

Sec. xv. Names proposed for membership to the Board shall be accompanied by the fee, and shall lie over one meeting before being acted upon, and then shall be subject to ballot.

AMENDMENTS.

Sec. xvi. These By-Laws may be altered or amended at any meeting of the Board, when a notice thereof, accompanied with the proposed alteration or amendment, shall have been submitted at a previous meeting.

ARTICLES OF INCORPORATION.

Know all Men by these Presents, That we, officers of the Iowa State Historical Society and members of its Board of Curators, by order of said Iowa State Historical Society, in order to increase the efficiency and secure the permanency of said Society, do hereby file in the office of the Recorder of deeds of Johnson county, of Iowa, these Articles of Incorporation, to the end that said Society may become Incorporated:

1. This Society shall be known under the name and by the appellation of the "Iowa State Historical Society."

2. Said Iowa State Historical Society shall be located permanently at the city of Iowa City, in the county of Johnson, in the said State of Iowa.

3. Said Society is organized and incorporated for the purpose of collecting, embodying, arranging and preserving, in authentic form, a library of books, pamphlets, maps, charts, manuscripts, papers, paintings, statuary and other materials illustrative of the history of the State of Iowa; to rescue from oblivion the memory of its early pioneers—to obtain and preserve narratives of their exploits, perils and hardy adventures; to secure facts and statements relative to the history, genius and progress, or decay, of our Indian tribes; and, also, to exhibit faithfully the antiquities, past and present resources of Iowa.

4. The officers of the said Society shall consist of a President, six Vice-Presidents, Corresponding Secretary, Treasurer and Librarian. Said officers shall perform the ordinary duties which their names respectively indicate.

5. The interests, business and control of said Society shall be vested in a Board of Curators—not less than eighteen in number—all of whom shall be members of said Society; and, said Board of Curators shall meet on the first Wednesday evening of each month, at the rooms of said Society, or of its Corresponding Secretary, for the transaction of such business, relative to the Society, as may require their attention.

6. The officers named in the two foregoing items shall be elected by the members of the Society, at a

meeting thereof, to be held at Iowa City on the first Tuesday in December of each year, and shall hold their offices for one year, and until their successors are duly elected and qualified.

7. The following persons shall act as officers of said Society until their successors are duly elected and qualified, to-wit:

President—Col. Wm. Penn Clark.
Vice-Presidents, 1st—Robert Hutchinson.
" 2nd—E. Price.
" 3rd—W. E. Miller.
" 4th—Z. C. Luse.
" 5th—John L. Davis.
" 6th—Theo. S. Parvin.
Corresponding Sec'y—Sanford W. Huff, M. D.
Recording Secretary—S. E. Paine.
Treasurer—H. S. Welton.
Librarian—C. F. Clark.

And said Board of Curators shall in like manner consist of the following persons, to-wit:

Col. S. C. Trowbridge,
Jno. P. Irish,
Prof. N. R. Leonard,
Wm. Vogt, M. D.,
Hon. F. H. Lee,
James R. Hartsock,
Samuel J. Hess,
Frederick Lloyd, M. D.,
Hon. Wm. H. Tuthill,
N. H. Brainerd,
Hon. Geo. W. McCleary,
Henry Murray, M. D.,
Wm. Crum,
W. C. Gaston, Esq.,
G. W. Dodder,
M. W. Davis,
Hon. Ralph P. Lowe,
Hon. George G. Wright.

And, until otherwise ordered, said Hon. Geo. W. McCleary shall remain and be President of said Board.

In witness whereof, we, members and officers of

said Society, hereunto subscribe our names this 6th day of November, A. D. 1867:

GEO. W. McCLEARY,
President Board of Curators.
SANFORD W. HUFF,
Corresponding Secretary.
F. H. LEE.
HENRY MURRAY, M. D.
S. C. TROWBRIDGE.
WILLIAM VOGT.
G. W. DODDER.
SAMUEL J. HESS.
M. W. DAVIS.
JNO. P. IRISH.
FREDERICK LLOYD.

Filed for record Dec. 2, 1867, at 3 o'clock P. M., and Recorded in Book 29, Page 381.

J. S. LODGE, Recorder.

ACTS

OF THE GENERAL ASSEMBLY OF IOWA RELATIVE TO THE IOWA STATE HISTORICAL SOCIETY.

An Act to provide for an annual appropriation for the benefit of a State Historical Society.

[Passed January 28, 1857, took effect July 4, 1857; Laws of Sixth General Assembly, Chapter 203, Page 337.]

SECTION 1959. (1.) Be it enacted by the General Assembly of the State of Iowa, That there is hereby annually appropriated until the Legislature shall by law otherwise direct, to a State Historical Society, formed or to be formed in connection with, and under the auspices of the State University, the sum of five hundred dollars,* to be expended by said Society in collecting, embodying, arranging and preserving in authentic form, a library of books, pamphlets, maps, charts, manuscripts, papers, paintings, statuary, and other materials illustrative of the state of the history of Iowa, to rescue from oblivion the memory of its early pioneers, to obtain and preserve varieties of their exploits, perils and hardy adventures; to secure facts and statements relative to the history, genius and progress or decay of our Indian tribes; to exhibit faithfully the antiquities, past and present resources of Iowa; also to aid in the publication of such of the collections of the Society as the Society shall from to time deem of value and interest, to aid in binding its books, pamphlets, manuscripts and papers, and in paying other necessary incidental expenses of the Society; but no part of such annual appropriation shall ever be paid for services rendered by the officers to the Society.

Sec. 1960. (2.) It shall be the duty of the Executive Committee of the said State Historical Society of Iowa to keep an accurate account of the manner of expenditure of the said sum of money hereby appropriated, and furnish the same, together with the vouchers thereof, to the Governor of this State, in the month of December of the year the Legislature shall meet, to be by him laid before the Legislature.

Sec. 1961. (3.) There shall be delivered to said Society thirty bound copies of all documents published by order of the State, for the purpose of effecting exchanges with similar Societies in other States, and also fifty bound copies of all such documents, to

* Section 1959 is thus amended by Section first of laws of Eighth General Assembly, Chapter 58, passed March 26, and took effect April 7, 1860. See special laws of Eighth Session, Page 146.

be transmitted through the medium of the Secretary of said Society, to M. Vattemere, at Paris, in furtherance of his system of International literary exchange.—Code Revision of 1860, Chapter 85.

An Act in relation to the State Historical Society by the Twelfth General Assembly, 1867–8.

WHEREAS, The Iowa State Historical Society was created by an act of the Sixth General Assembly of the State of Iowa, for the purpose of collecting, arranging and preserving books, pamphlets, maps, charts, manuscripts, papers, paintings, statuary, and other materials illustrative of the history of this State; and, also, to preserve the memory of the early pioneers of Iowa, their deeds, exploits, perils and adventures; to secure facts relative to the history of our Indian tribes; to exhibit faithfully the antiquities, and to mark the progress of our rapidly developing Commonwealth; to publish such of the collections of the Society as it shall from time to time deem of value and interest; to bind such publications and other books, pamphlets, manuscripts and papers, as they may publish or collect; and to aid in all respects, as may be within its province, to develope the history of this State in all its departments; thereof,

SECTION 1. Be it enacted by the General Assembly of the State of Iowa, For the above purposes, and to aid in defraying the incidental expenses of said Society, including rent and salary of the Secretary, there is hereby appropriated out of any money in the State Treasury not otherwise appropriated, the sum of three thousand dollars per annum for two years, to be drawn on the order, and expended by, the Board of Curators of the said State Historical Society, in such sums as they may from time to time require.

SEC. 2. It shall be the duty of said Society to keep an accurate account of the manner of expenditure of the money hereby appropriated, and furnish a full statement thereof, together with the vouchers, to the Governor of this State, in the month of December preceding the meeting of each session of the General Assembly, to be by him laid before it.

SEC. 3. There shall be delivered to the said Society eighty (80) bound copies of all books and documents published by order of the State, for the purpose of effecting exchanges with similar Societies in other States, and for preservation in the library of said Society.

SEC. 4. All acts and parts of acts inconsistent with this act are hereby repealed.

SEC. 5. This act being deemed of immediate importance, shall be in force from and after its publication in the Daily State Register and Iowa Evening Statesman, newspapers published at Des Moines.

Approved April 7, 1868.

STATE OF IOWA,
OFFICE OF SECRETARY OF STATE,
DES MOINES, Apr. 11, 1868.

I hereby certify the foregoing to be a true copy of the original roll now on file in this office.

ED WRIGHT, Sec. of State.

www.ingramcontent.com/pod-product-compliance
Lightning Source LLC
LaVergne TN
LVHW020637110826
845149LV00004B/1239

* 9 7 8 1 4 1 8 1 9 0 9 5 8 *